Fore
Mark,
Merry Christmas
Lore - Mom

For my dad and his love of the game

Endpaper and title page art
copyright © 1998 B. Brent Atwater
Original interior artwork
copyright © 1998 Wendy Wegner,
licensed by Wild Apple Licensing

Designed by Arlene Greco

Copyright © 1998
Peter Pauper Press, Inc.
202 Mamaroneck Avenue
White Plains, NY 10601
All rights reserved
ISBN 0-88088-071-6
Printed in China
7 6 5 4 3 2 1

Master Strokes

Golf Pros on the Game

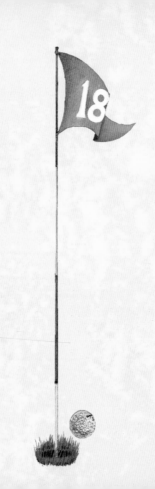

Contents

The Inner Game

Play picture golf. Try to see the
line and see the ball going into
the hole. Try to keep this picture in your mind. It's a form
of self-hypnosis. You're more
than halfway to putting it in.

Bruce Crampton

You have to have the strength
of will not to mess around
with what you've been taught
or what you've already proved
is right for you.

George Archer

The trick . . . is to stay serene. The whole secret of mastering the game of golf—and this applies to the beginner as well as to the pro—is to cultivate a mental approach to the game which will enable you to shrug off bad shots, shrug off bad days, keep patient and know in your heart that sooner or later you will be back on top....

Arnold Palmer

You're completely alone with every conceivable opportunity to defeat yourself.

Hale Irwin

The best ways I know to com-
bat tension are to do deep
knee bends on the tee, or
shake your hands vigorously
before taking the shot. That
gets the blood flowing again
and loosens the knots.

Jane Blalock

It's amazing how delicate the
game is... There's a huge
difference between hoping
you'll play well and knowing
you'll play well.

Mike Donald

[Y]ou need some guidelines
. . . But fit those guidelines to
your physical and mental
makeup. Then practice to
refine and improve.

Tom Kite

A successful golfer continual-
ly adds to his resources. Even
when you get down to a sin-
gle-figure handicap, it pays to
remain alert for any chance of
advancing your golfing educa-
tion.

Bruce Devlin

The only thing that gets in the way of a golfer's success is the golfer himself: whether he can make a good swing at the ball, which is a matter of mechanics, or whether he has the good sense of where the right place is to aim a shot, which is a matter of strategy. Golf is a game of next shots and the preparation or setting up of them.

Billy Casper

Golf is a non-violent game
played violently from within.

Bob Toski

The traditions of the game
are rich with memories of
dramatic triumphs as well as
heartbreaking failures. The
best players fail the most
because they are in the hunt
all the time. You learn to han-
dle it—accept it or you don't
survive . . . I've been out
there and I know.

Deane Beman

On the golf course, a man may be the dogged victim of inexorable fate, be struck down by an appalling stroke of tragedy, become the hero of a side-splitting comedy—any of these within a few hours, and all without having to bury a corpse or repair a tangled personality.

Bobby Jones

[T]here've been a lot of times I've wanted to strangle a club or two of my own. How about you?

Lee Trevino

Winning golf is a matter of touch. It's something you work at and try to develop, but you don't develop it. It just comes to you. . . . Once you've got the touch you're set. Even if you make a bad shot now and then, you know you've still got it. The good golfer has got the touch, he knows he can do it.

Ben Hogan

I hate this game. And I can't wait till tomorrow to play it again.

Jeff Sluman

[T]here's always the individual challenge of making the ball do what you want it to. That's what keeps me going. That's why golf is an art form.

Dave Hill

The simpler I keep things, the better I play. Try to keep that in mind, especially if you are just taking up the game. Trust your instincts. Find a swing that feels comfortable and works for you and then practice until you can groove that swing.

Nancy Lopez

[I]mprovement in golf just never follows a straight upward path. Do not despair when the poorer rounds come. Remember that the pleasure lies in conquering the tough problems. Stay with it. You will begin again to improve. And this time (maybe) you will remember not to be too exultant, too proud. Then you will REALLY be learning the game.

Cary Middlecoff

Golf is the hardest game in the world. There's no way you can ever get it. Just when you think you do, the game jumps up and puts you into your place.

Ben Crenshaw

It's amazing when you don't try, you just look at it and hit it, how much better you do, rather than thinking about everything that can go right or wrong. Just let your instincts take over. That was a perfect shot.

Davis Love III

There's no better feeling in the world than . . . to be able to hit that ball within a foot and a half of where you want to hit it. That's what the pinnacle is all about. You don't get that all the time, but when you get it, there's nobody else in the world who can experience what you're experiencing. You have control over yourself. You have control over your mind. . . .

Greg Norman

[M]ental images can be plant-
ed in the brain—particularly
by the golfer himself, which is
self-needling. Playing with
Jim Turnesa one day, I was
intently studying his actions
on the tee. Turnesa pushed
his drive into timber to the
right. The image of everything
Turnesa had done was so
strong in my mind that I
stepped up and my muscles
followed the image and I did
the same thing, landing
almost exactly in the same
spot in the jungle as had Jim.
After that, I watched my
opponents only casual-like.

Sam Snead

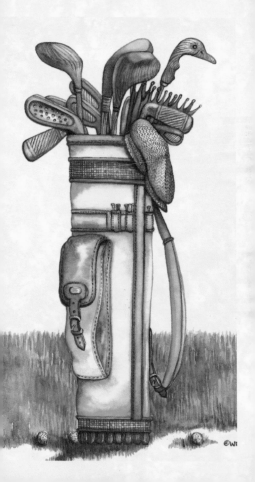

I've always dreamed of coming up 18 and winning. But I never thought this far through the ceremony.

Tiger Woods

I've always looked at the form of the game as one where the player could blend with nature . . . where one could create beautiful shots that matched the beauty of the surroundings.

Dean Lind

If you build your golfing house on a sound foundation, you will always derive pleasure from the game.

Johnny Miller

Golf may be . . . a sophisticated game. At least, it is usually played with the outward appearance of great dignity. It is, nevertheless, a game of considerable passion, either of the explosive type, or that which burns inwardly and sears the soul.

Bobby Jones

If you can manage, you don't have to be the world's greatest golfer. You need to organize yourself mentally and physically. . . . You strive for an edge, then management will hold that edge for you.

Ben Hogan

Golf requires a technique that none of us ever quite master, but which we all think we could master with just a little more playing and a little more practice.

Tony Lema

I've got a mental advantage out there. Not because I'm smarter. Just because I realize what the mind can do. You can get some fantastic results by programming your subconscious. I'm serious.

Johnny Miller

You beat yourself when you start playing the other fellow rather than the golf course. . . . Play the golf course, not your opponent. . . . [C]oncentrate on your game, not his.

Bob Zender

Occasionally you'll have some bad luck, but you get it the other way around too, you get some bad shots that turn out good. You have to play well over a long period of time.

Tom Sieckman

[G]olf is always a trip back to the first tee, the more you play the more you realize you are staying where you are.

Shivas Irons

Golf is a game, and as such it is meant to be enjoyed. This is the first principle that the new golfer should understand. Golf can be a vivid test of your emotions and skill. But never let the test become so serious that you lose sight of the fact that enjoyment is your number one goal.

Gary Wiren

Golf is a game more full of variables than most. It's never the same, and you're always learning. The golf course changes, you change, the weather changes, your playing partners change, your goals change—but the challenge remains the same. It's you against the course—and that little white ball.

Judy Rankin

I'll guarantee that you can take the swing you have right now and improve your handicap by simply paying attention to the other factors involved in playing golf—your short game, your strategic approach, your emotional control.

Tom Kite

All seasoned players know, or at least have felt, that when you are playing your best, you are much the same as in a state of meditation. You are free of tension and chatter. You are concentrating on one thing. It is the ideal condition for good golf.

Harvey Penick

Perhaps the desire to improve
is greater in golfers than in
any other sportsmen, possi-
bly because there are other
opponents besides your fel-
low-competitor. There is the
constant battle against par
and the even greater struggle
within yourself.

Gary Player

All golfers are peers.

Thorvald MacDougal

Master Strokes

Golf, more than most games,
has a number of clichés, often
successfully disguised as
"tips."

Kathy Whitworth

It is nothing new or original
to say that golf is played one
stroke at a time. But it took
me many years to realize it.

Bobby Jones

All golfers, men and women, professional and amateur, are united by one thing: their desire to improve. That's one of the great things about playing . . . —you're always learning how to get better.

Judy Rankin

The point of golf is to get command of a swing which the more pressure you put on it, the better it works.

Ben Hogan

Try to think of your golf swing as an efficient machine. Each part of it is dependent upon the other parts; if one part is functioning incorrectly the others will be affected. But working together they deliver the same effective result time after time. . . Build the most efficient machine you can. You'll be surprised how much more enjoyable the game will be if you do.

Julius Boros

If a person could just forget the ball is there and swing the clubhead smoothly through that spot, he would hit many more good shots. I've seen thousands of players who take a great practice swing and then make an atrocious pass at the ball. They ought to hit the ball with their practice swings.

Dave Hill

Make no mistake, grooving a swing that repeats itself should be your *top* priority.

Fred Couples

I focus on a shot—like the three-wood on number one at Olympic with out-of-bounds behind the hole, I aimed it right. There was a dead tree behind the green and the tree was just smack in the middle of the green. I aimed at the right-hand edge of a dead branch. I didn't aim at the tree, I aimed at a point on the branch of a tree. I could see a little knot on the branch and focused on that.

Greg Norman

So far as I'm concerned, you can toss all the "tips" into the garbage can. The only way to play consistently good golf is through the mastery of a set of basics that the great players of the past have proved to be integral to the swing.

Jack Grout

A driver is the key to the golf round—the key that starts your car, the key that opens your house. Without a good driver, you're not going to put the ball down in the middle of the fairway.

Lee Trevino

The most exquisitely satisfying act in the world of golf is that of throwing a club. The full backswing, the delayed wrist action, the flowing follow-through, followed by that unique whirring sound, reminiscent only of a flock of passing starlings, is without parallel in sport.

Henry Longhurst

The secret is to be versatile. Experiment and never stop learning. Golf is a continual learning process. . . . Play around with clubs. Learn the extraordinary range of shots you can play with any one club. Hit it high, hit it low, bend it this way and that. Develop feel and wonderful ball control and with it the true art of good scoring.

Nick Faldo

Swinging a club is such an
unnatural move that imitating
someone who hits the ball
well can be an easy way to
learn. You can watch someone and say to yourself, "I
don't follow through like she
does." And so you try to do
what she does.

Beth Daniel

I have always maintained that golf is a simple game: Bring the club up, bring the club down, bring the club through. *Swing through* the ball, don't *hit* at it. When you execute a proper golf swing, the ball just happens to get in the way of the clubhead.

Walter Ostroske

To develop a good repeating swing, you need concentrate only on timing and balance and rhythm. On paper, this *is* simple. However, in the pursuit of pleasure while playing golf, whether for fun or funds, the human element comes into it all the time, and this complicates the best of methods.

Bob Charles

The type of stroke used is important to the success of the chip shot, but judgment about where on the green to aim for and about club loft is at least as important as the shot itself. If a player works on his judgment he should find that he can become very skilled around the greens and that his scores will drop.

Earl Stewart

The distance your ball travels is governed solely by the amount of power you unleash at impact. . . . "[S]wing easy and hit hard." . . . You can't play golf well unless you know the right movements and why these movements will contribute to a sound swing. You immediately handicap yourself on the course with less.

Julius Boros

Swing the club back slowly, like you're doing a waltz—da, da, da, da, da. . . . The first step to slowing down, to putting some musical rhythm into your swing and not just muscling everything, is to take a relaxed grip. . . . [J]ust swing back slowly, count to yourself, hear that waltz music, do anything that relaxes you. . . . [S]top at the top of the swing, and pull the club down with your left hand with elastic wrists. . . . Just swing nice 'n' easy. Slowly, slowly, slowly! This is the way to hitting the ball far . . .

Sam Snead

Hitting the ball straight has always been my main priority, and I'm convinced that just keeping the ball in play is the average player's key to lower scores.

Fred Funk

When you stop throwing away strokes needlessly, you start to play winning golf. . . . It is the quickest route I know to success on the golf course.

Bob Zender

You've missed shots. So have I. So have other mortals. When are we going to realize that missing simple shots is part of being humans? But there are worse things than missing golf shots. . . . When we learn to adjust ourselves to the good and the bad shots, we have learned one of the lessons of golf that is far beyond golf.

Tommy Armour

[A]ll that matters to the ball is what your clubhead does to it. Your shots, for good or bad, are determined by your impact conditions. . . . I would suggest that you never accept a piece of instruction, no matter how enticing, without first asking just how this advice will improve your clubhead's impact with the ball.

John Jacobs

[D]on't pretend you're Jack Nicklaus. You're not.

Bob Zender

I have . . . top action—I use the upper half of my body. When I'm swinging my arms and turning my shoulders on the backswing, I feel I'm winding up like a spring. The spring tightens and tightens until I can feel the strain in my upper body. Then all that tension releases in the down-swing.

Nancy Lopez

I ask a golfer to take a practice swing and try to hit the ground hard enough to make a mark. Then I measure the distance between the mark and the end of his toes. That's where he should be standing when there's a ball there.

Robert Cloughan

It doesn't much matter what kind of clubhead is on one end of that shiny metal shaft if a fat head is on the other.

Robinson Murray

My father taught me. . . . I remember he put my hands on the club and said, "That's the way you hold it." He said it just once, but that was enough. I have held it that way from then on.

Arnold Palmer

Time and time again I have seen a player face a difficult shot that he decides he wants to play safe. He may shorten his swing, slow down his usual tempo and just punch the ball toward safety. . . The very fact that he has changed

Putting Around

Very early in my career I realized that putting was half the game of golf. No matter how well I might play the long shots, if I could not putt I would never win.

Bobby Locke

What I have to do now is learn to control my emotions, cope with the Sunday jitters, and stop getting down on myself after every missed putt.

Tommy Tolles

I know a lot of the tour pros think exactly the opposite to me about the putting stroke. That's fine. They are using what they have discovered works for them. So am I. And so should every golfer.

George Archer

You can always recover from a bad drive, but there's no recovering from a bad putt. It's missing those 6-inchers that causes guys to break up their sticks.

Jimmy Demaret

It has become habitual on both the men's and women's tours to mark the ball after the first putt. This is more a psychological gimmick than anything else. I strongly urge the club golfer to walk up and finish the putt, eliminating the needless delay and tension. It will not only speed up play, it will make you a better putter.

Jane Blalock

Hitting a golf ball and putting have nothing in common. They're two different games. You work all your life to perfect a repeating swing that will get you to the greens, and then you have to try to do something that is totally unrelated. There shouldn't be any cups, just flag sticks. And then the man who hit the most fairways and greens and got closest to the pins would be the tournament winner.

Ben Hogan

In all golf shots, the important factor in success is to achieve a tempo or rhythm similar to that of a clock's pendulum. The hands can alter this tempo according to the shot required, but to maintain control of the club it must be moved at uniform speed.

Don't forget that these shots are holeable and are just as important as long putts. Here again, one should carefully examine the area eight to ten feet from the hole.

Bruce Devlin

The idea of golf is to get the ball in the hole. Since the green is where the hole is, that's the place where emotion is ultimately released, or expressed. When a player holes a crucial short putt, or rolls one in from sixty feet, it is on the green—on the "dance floor," as golfers like to say—where he punches the air and does a little jig of celebration.

Al Barkow